Rob Walker

WINTER AWAKENINGS

Illustrated by Anita Bagdi

First paperback edition published in 2022

Book design by Anita Bagdi

Printed in the UK

WINTER AWAKENINGS

Chapter 1

Just a short dream from where you are right now, there's a certain, rather special place. Not so much a town as a village; not so much a village as a train of tiny homes snaking quaintly around the twists and turns of a little lane.

And on a tall hill, on the outskirts of this little scene, stands a circle of trees. From the oldest and tallest to the youngest and shortest, they huddle together, nestling behind their branches, a secret play place waiting to be discovered by each new child who happens to pass through.

Every year, the winter's snow faithfully visits this place, its guest for a few precious weeks. Like a favourite uncle, the children long for its arrival. And as if hearing their call, on a certain night it whispers down and waits playfully, smooth and even on the ground, a blanket of white draped lovingly over the entire scene, as far as your imagination can see.

As the children open their curtains, the gift is unwrapped and beheld; a whole new world, right where the old world was, foreign and new, whiter than white, waiting to be explored. And beyond, in the distance on the hill, the circle of trees call kids to come, to run, to roll down its banks, to bring sleighs and all instruments of play, and to stay for as long as the day will allow.

Scarcely has the sun yawned its first breath when the first door is flung open. As more eyes meet the snow, young smiles tumble clumsily from front doors, children flinging themselves onto the earth's belly, now soft and white. Then, as if all gripped at once by the same idea, they grab whatever they can and make toward the trees, toward the promise of a winter wonderland on the banks behind their branches.

And from here on, all the days in wonderland merge into one, and become the stuff of their dreams during the nights in-between. Anything that slides is a sleigh on the banks: the lid of a dustbin, an old plastic sack. Blades on skaters' shoes cut along the river, now frozen in its tracks by the chill of winter's breath. Snowballs of all sizes become the traffic of the air.

Sadly, each year the snow never lingers too long, but gives its dose in drops, lest people's taste for it dwindle. And so Christmas being over, the New Year begun, the school bell calls time on the pleasure and fun. Snowmen are left, sleighs are deserted, in droves they return to their homes.

One year, all but three little children remained in the basin, unable to let the marvel of their wonderland go once more.

Two brothers and a little sister named Alice were putting the finishing touches to their beloved sculptures. ‘Snowmen’ seemed too small a word to describe their cherished creations.

The figures were drawn in the very image of their creators: two snowboys and a snowgirl. As Alice and her two older brothers stood back and looked at their work they smiled, and little Alice shed a tear. They all knew that the figures could never last. Unwilling to spoil such splendour and take back the scarves and glasses they’d given them, they decided to leave them right where they were.

The brothers took a final look before turning and heading back toward home. Alice stayed for a moment, long enough to kiss the snowy figures goodbye and whisper to them that she wished she could have given them real breath and real lives.

Finally she dragged herself away and followed her brothers, casting a last look over her shoulder as she went.

The circle of trees surrounding the scene stood silently, still. They seemed to sigh, almost to mourn, with branches downcast, quietly longing for the return of young noise to their palm.

Then, suddenly struck by a thought, they looked again at the snowmen, and with Alice's words still echoing in their branches they couldn't resist. Desperate to join in, to be part of the game, they decided to donate just an ounce of their spirit. As they lifted up their branches and jointly exhaled, a little of their essence left them, travelled along the snowy ground and up through the figures, so delicately made.

For a moment there was nothing; a moment longer, still nothing. The three snowy figures seemed unmoved by the magic.

Then all of a sudden, whilst nothing else stirred, the snowgirl's acorn eyes appeared to shift in their sockets, looking around with a quizzical wonder, mystified and a little afraid.

Shortly after this, the eyes of another, this time with spectacles, right beside her, began to do the same. Two pairs of eyes now roamed all directions, trying to make sense of the scene that surrounded them.

From the corner of one eye, the head wearing glasses spotted the other and turned towards her, then she turned towards his.

One pair of eyes met another.

Finally, the spectacled one's mouth began to form a shape, as if ready to make a sound, and before he could stop it, a word came tumbling out.

“Hello.”

His eyes grew wide with alarm, unable to believe it was him. He peered to the other and found the snowgirl looking equally frightened. His eyes tried to apologise but struggled to cope with the task. Before he knew it, his mouth was again starting to shape itself into doing something ,and then, from out of nowhere:

“Sorry, I think that was me.”

He looked at her, embarrassed, then stared down at his mouth to see if it had finished. By looking down and going almost cross-eyed, he could just about see his mouth, which seemed to be where the words had come from.

Eager to explore this a bit more, he started to move it in all directions, opening and closing it before finally puckering up his lips and loudly blowing an enormous raspberry.

The snowgirl stared at him strangely.

“They just come out. I have a thought, then they all come out. Like now, like this.”

The snowgirl said nothing, but looked on with a puzzled expression.

“Can you do it?” he asked.

The snowgirl pondered, as if this were the first thought ever to enter her snowy head, but her mouth was somehow ahead of her.

“I don’t know...”

Her eyes jumped, this time at the sound of her own voice. She stared ahead with eyes wide, seized with fear.

Finally, she managed to breathe out, before timidly whispering,

“Yes... it seems I can.”

The one in spectacles looked relieved for a second, but then his confusion returned.

“Who are you?” he asked.

“I don’t know” she replied. “Who are you?”

“I don’t know either” he admitted.

“Have you got a name?” she asked, as though not even sure what this meant.

“Probably” he said.

“Have I?” she continued hopefully.

“Who knows?” he replied, talking as much to himself as to her.

“Who does know?” she thought, asking herself the same question.

Then, out of nowhere and without his consent, the one in spectacles felt one of his legs moving out to take a step.

“How did you do that?” exclaimed the snowgirl in disbelief.

“I don’t know” he replied, shocked. “I just thought we should find out what’s going on, and off it went!”

“Can you do it again?” she asked.

He took a deep breath and thought as hard as he could. Slowly and surely the leg moved again, this time with more life in it than before. Soon the snowgirl had got the idea too, and the two of them practised going forward then backward, one after the other, each new step making them laugh louder than the last.

Very soon they discovered that their arms and hands could move as well, so both of them soon found themselves dancing around in the snow and having a ball. All of sudden, the snowgirl saw something behind her new friend that stopped her heart, cold.

Noticing her worried expression, the one in spectacles turned to find a third figure in the snow that they hadn't even noticed until now, right beside them. They peered at the figure, but he seemed listless, lifeless, still and cold.

"Do you think he's like us?" asked the one in spectacles, nervously.

"What are we like?" replied the snowgirl.

He stopped and thought. "I don't know."

They tapped the third figure in snow, but not one part of him flinched... nothing. They tapped him harder, but still he remained lifeless. Determined not to give up, the one in spectacles then got in very close and shouted "Hello!" loudly, pretty much in the poor thing's face. The eyes of the third figure burst open suddenly, alarmed and afraid.

"Who are you?" he barked, looking terribly anxious. Both jumped back in fright.

"We don't know" said the snowgirl.

"We thought you might" added the one in spectacles.

The third snowman looked about himself nervously, as if rudely awakened from a long sleep.

"Where am I?" he said to himself.

After a pause, the snowgirl timidly offered the only suggestion she could think of.

"Here?"

"Where was I before, though?" asked the third figure.

The other two shrugged. The new figure in snow continued to stand there, thinking hard.

"Was I before?"

The snowgirl and her friend looked at each other, struggling to know how to help their poor new companion.

"Before when?" asked the one in spectacles.

"Now" said the third figure.

"Sorry. We can't help" said the snowgirl, her face displaying her most sorry expression.

"We were only just before you" added her friend.

The new arrival now seemed even more confused.

"Did you arrive together?"

"Sort of... I think" offered the snowgirl.

"Someone must know what's going on" huffed and puffed this last figure as he awakened, looking rather unamused. For the first time he seemed to look properly at his two new friends.

Suddenly they all realised they had no names. They didn't even know their own names, let alone the names of the other two. The new arrival decided that the one in glasses should be called Specs, his spectacles of course being the only thing found on him, apart from a carrot for his nose – and no one wants to be called Carrot.

The snowgirl managed to find a name on the label of the new arrival's scarf, etched on with pen: "Oliver Jones". And so the new arrival declared himself to be called Ollie and looked absolutely made up, saying it to himself in as many different ways as he could.

Finally they had to agree on a name for the poor snowgirl, who by now was feeling rather left out. Both of her new friends seemed altogether happier now that they had names, but she, poor thing, had none. Specs searched her beautiful silk scarf for another name etched in pen, but instead found an extra special-looking label with the word LIBERTY stitched into it in big gold letters, and underneath, in smaller gold letters, "London".

The two boys declared her name to be Liberty and felt very privileged, as they assumed from her fancy scarf with gold lettering that she must be a princess. Liberty decided she'd like to assume that too.

Chapter 2

With introductions made, the three decided on a plan.

“Ollie’s right” said Liberty. “Someone must know what’s going on” she said, staring out into the distance. “There’s certainly nothing this way, just white, white and more white.”

“Maybe there’s something over that bank!” suggested Ollie, suddenly much more hopeful. “Up by those trees. We’ll be able to see for miles from up there.”

“That’s a brilliant idea” said Specs. “We must be able to see some clues from up there.”

“That’s agreed then” said Ollie. “We’ll climb it.”

“Climb it?” asked Liberty, a little uneasily. “It’s very steep.”

Smiling, Specs offered her his hand. Then, with Ollie leading the way, the three new friends began to venture up the snowy bank. It was much longer and harder than they thought it would be. When you’ve only just learnt you have legs, not to mention can walk, each new step feels almost like a whole journey in itself.

Halfway up, poor Ollie slipped and almost tumbled right back down again, but luckily Specs managed to catch him with his other arm. His first arm, of course, was already in use, clutching hold of poor Liberty, who didn't look very happy.

“Are we nearly at the top?” she asked hopefully.

“I think we’re halfway up” Ollie told her confidently.

“My legs hurt” whined Specs.

“A stick!” shouted Ollie suddenly, before excitedly grabbing a long, thin fallen branch from a few paces in front of him. He tore off the smaller branches, leaving him with a pretty decent-looking cane.

“Is that good?” remarked Specs. “What does that tell us?”

“Nothing” said Ollie. “It’s just good for helping me up this hill.”

“Oh” said Specs, a little disappointed.

The three continued to struggle up the steep bank. Ollie, with his new stick, was managing to cover the ground a little quicker than Specs and Liberty. Finally he reached the top and peered out over the edge of the basin. Specs and Liberty watched him reach the summit and called out excitedly.

“Well?” shouted Specs.

“What’s up there?” shouted Liberty.

Ollie wasn’t moving. He just stood and stared, apparently transfixed. Specs and Liberty looked at each other in confusion. Liberty shrugged her shoulders. They journeyed on and finally joined Ollie at the top. As they looked out over the edge of the basin, their faces slowly dropped. The mystery of their awakening deepened as they beheld their new universe as far as their eyes could see. It gave no further clues. For a few seconds no one seemed able to speak.

“I think I need new glasses” said Specs. “All I can see is white.”

“You don’t need new glasses” advised Ollie with a downcast face.

“White, white and more white” said Liberty finally, in a solemn tone.

Specs tried his best to keep their spirits up. He noticed the circle of trees right beside them and shouted up to them.

“Ah… hello there.”

Not a word did they speak. Undeterred, he tried again: “Any idea what’s going on?”

The circle of trees remained as silent as the cold air that raged between them. You’d have thought the trees, on seeing their distress, might have offered them a hint. But the play being staged in the palm of their hand was too precious to spoil.

Specs looked down, his heart full of disappointment for an instant, only to be lifted a moment later by the sight of two little rabbits springing from behind the trees. On seeing the snow figures, they stopped in their tracks and twitched their little noses, as if trying to sniff out whether they meant danger. With their cautious eyes fixed on the new strangers, the little rabbits did nothing but stare, poised and alert, waiting for one of them to make a move.

Specs eventually decided to try and greet them properly, but as soon as he took one little step toward them, the rabbits hopped off hurriedly down the bank and away.

“Oh no… don’t go!” called Specs, chasing after them. “We don’t know where… we don’t know what… we don’t know who…”

But it was too late. The rabbits had disappeared into the distance. As Specs sighed and gazed forlornly after them, it wasn’t long before he heard Ollie shouting to him. He turned around to see him pointing to the tops of the trees, where a whole flock of birds had just landed.

Specs ran back and shouted up to them for help.

“Hello!”

But the birds were so engrossed in their own private chatter that over their ceaseless squawking, not a single one even heard poor Specs, who to them was just a little dot way down there on the ground. Desperate to be noticed, Specs shook a branch madly to attract their attention, but instead of this helping, the birds were simply startled and flew abruptly away, leaving the snow friends on their own again.

“Do you think they know?” asked Liberty.

“Know what?” asked Specs.

“How we are, of course.”

"Are what? Here?" Ollie replied.

"Just *are*."

"I suppose now we'll never know" said Ollie.

Still holding the branch, Specs then noticed a third creature of the animal kingdom, on a leaf not far beyond the end of his nose. It was the most beautiful little emerald green caterpillar. The poor little chap looked like he'd been left behind.

Next to him on the leaf, and on more leaves nearby, were numerous little cocoons in which lots of other caterpillars seemed to be warmly preparing their wings, looking like they'd been there for months. But this particular little one seemed to have been left out in the cold. As Specs continued to hold the leaf, eventually the caterpillar crawled onto his hand and seemed almost to stare at them all, now gathered around in wonder at the sight.

"What is it?" whispered Ollie, cautiously. Then he whispered again "Are you going to ask it?"

"I suppose so" said Specs, looking a little nervous, because for all he knew, whatever he was holding in the palm of his hand might have answers to all their questions. He cleared his throat and began.

"Hello. We've just arrived here. We don't know who we are, what we are, where we came from or where we're going. Can you help?"

The three waited with bated breath. They waited, and they waited, and they waited. At one point the caterpillar looked up as if he might be about to speak, but then he buried his nose again, as if trying to locate the leaf that he was certain he'd been on only a short while ago.

Sadly, it became clear that the caterpillar wasn't going to help very much, so Specs gently placed him back on the leaf and the three looked at each other, each hoping the other had a new plan.

For what seemed like an age, the three of them stood helplessly at the top of the basin, staring out at the universe of white surrounding them, a universe that seemed to offer no clues to the source of their awakening. With the mystery starting to exhaust them a little, Specs and Liberty decided to rest their weary backs against the solid trunk of the oldest-looking tree. There was something about the thick trunk that seemed loving and wise and made them almost want to embrace it.

Eventually Ollie came out of the mood that had been eating away at him and looked across at the other two... and then beyond them. Something had caught his eye. He strode past Specs and Liberty with an unusual spring in his step. Specs looked to Liberty for a clue. Liberty shrugged. Suddenly he called out from behind them:

"Look!"

They turned around to see that he'd found a metal dustbin lid, minus a handle, that someone before them had clearly been using as a sleigh.

"What is it?" asked Liberty, hopefully.

"Who knows?" said Ollie.

"It's something" said Specs.

"It's definitely something" said Ollie.

"Does it tell us what's going on?" asked Liberty. There was a long pause before anyone wanted to answer. Ollie held it up.

"I don't think it's ever going to do that."

"Well then, what use is it" said Liberty, clearly as a statement rather than a question. And with this, she sulkily resumed her sitting position against the tree, with her back to them. Ollie took his new-found treasure over to her and gave her a cheeky smile.

"I'll show you what use it is."

And with this, he jumped on it and cascaded down the snowy bank at a hundred miles an hour.

"Weeeee!!!!" and he'd gone.

The other two looked amazed.

"How did he know it did that?" asked Liberty.

"I don't know" said Specs. "But it does." Then he added quickly "And I'm next."

In a trice, the two were arguing over who should go next, and of course Specs, being a true gentleman, let Liberty go before him – or, to be more precise, not before him but in front of him. Not wanting to go down the hill on her own to start with, she grasped Specs' arm as Ollie hauled the sleigh back up the hill, firmly letting him know that she wanted to sit right behind him. So once Ollie had finally reached them and managed to stop talking about his thrilling maiden voyage down the bank, eager to experience it for themselves, Liberty and Specs arranged themselves as neatly as they could on the sleigh before teetering on the edge and allowing Ollie to gently push them off.

Chapter 3

Their shrieks of delight and wonder echoed first for hours, then for days, and eventually for weeks on end within the borders of the basin, a new life that had all started with their discovery of the abandoned dustbin lid. Sleigh riding became easier and easier as their legs got stronger and stronger. Soon even Specs and Liberty were able to ascend to the top of the bank in record time, especially when it was their turn to sleigh down again.

But this was only the beginning. Next came Specs' discovery of the frozen river, with patterns on the surface made by the twirling blades of skaters' shoes. In wonder they tried to imagine what kind of ancestors could possibly have carved these strange icy pictures for them. This wonder was soon overtaken by the thrilling discovery of skating, shoe-less, on the river's surface. This provided at least a further week's new-found entertainment. Ollie always led the way out in front, while Specs and Liberty, more cautious in nature, were usually behind, looking after each other but enjoying it just as much.

In a special little ceremony to mark their beloved basin as home, using a flint Ollie had found, they etched their names into the bark at the bottom of the trunk of their favourite tree. Around their names they scratched a heart shape, symbolising their love for each other and for their beautiful home.

And all this time their adventures were silently observed, absorbed and enjoyed by the circle of trees, their branches seeming almost to nudge each other subtly as the three friends discovered each new thing in the world surrounding them.

They seemed to have completely forgotten about trying to resolve who and what they were and from where they had come. As no clues were forthcoming, they just got on with having fun, with apparently endless distractions to keep them from dwelling on what their minds couldn't fathom. However, often, in the dead of night as they huddled together under the trees, each one still silently wondered why on earth they had been brought to life, and who or what lay behind it all. For each of them, this thought sent an uneasy ripple through their snowy bodies.

One day, after a week or more of days when the chill in the air seemed distinctly milder and the brightness around them stronger, while Ollie skated on the frozen river, Specs and Liberty were by the trees, peering at the leaf where they had seen the caterpillar only a few weeks previously. An unusual transformation seemed to be taking place. The little thing had begun to spin a silky cocoon around himself and was gradually disappearing from their sight, immersing himself in his cosy little sleeping bag, until pretty soon he would be entirely inside it, head and all.

They would have enquired where he was going and whether they would see their little friend again, but by now they knew that, for whatever reason, the many creatures around them, in the air and on the ground, didn't want to or didn't know how to talk to them. What they found most curious about the other inhabitants of their world was that they all seemed to know their place there and appeared perfectly at peace with it all. This made them feel as though they simply must be missing something.

Just then, from below on the frozen river they heard Ollie let out a yelp. They ran down the bank and across to him, only to find that their poor friend had managed to put his foot straight through the ice into the water below. Not only that: even more surprising, he suddenly seemed to be missing a foot.

"What on earth happened to you?" asked Specs, anxiously.

"It took my foot" said Ollie.

"What did?" cried Liberty, looking about her, afraid.

"That!" said Ollie, pointing to the water, now visible through the gaping hole in the ice.

Specs and Liberty peered into the water, fascinated by this new discovery, but also very afraid.

“What is that?” whispered Liberty, with increasing curiosity.

“I don’t know, but it took my foot!” said Ollie angrily. “I was skating along, and all of a sudden my foot went straight through into that stuff. When I took it out, it had gone.”

“Gosh” said Liberty, with some surprise.

“It looks so harmless” said Specs, as he bravely put his nose even closer to the hole made by Ollie’s foot. He could now see the water even more clearly as the gentle breeze created tiny ripples on its surface.

“Are you sure it’s taken your foot for good?” said Specs. “I can’t imagine something so pretty meaning to do you any harm.”

“What on earth do you mean?” said Ollie, defensively. “You can see my foot has gone!”

“Maybe it just fell off” suggested Liberty. “Maybe if we find it, we can put it back on” she added.

“I bet it’s right there just beneath the surface” said Specs, confidently. And with this, he knelt down right by the hole in the ice, and prepared to delve in with his arm to retrieve Ollie’s leg.

“Be careful!” shouted Ollie.

“Yes, do be careful” added Liberty.

“Whatever that stuff is, it has teeth” Ollie warned him.

“Did it feel like your leg was being bitten off?” asked Specs.

“Not exactly” admitted Ollie.

“Well then” said Specs, “it probably wasn’t.”

And with this, he very carefully put his arm into the water and started to delve around, trying to locate Ollie’s missing foot.

After a minute or so, Ollie and Liberty couldn't help but notice what appeared to be a very relaxed, calm little smile emerging on Specs' face.

"Have you got it?" Ollie asked excitedly.

"No, not yet" said Specs.

"Well then, why are you smiling?" demanded Ollie, feeling a little at odds.

"Because it feels awfully nice and... strangely familiar" said Specs. "It's warm, and when it's all around you, it's like nothing else I can think of."

"Are you still looking?" Ollie asked impatiently.

"Oh yes, sorry" said Specs. "Let me try with my other arm. Maybe I could delve a little deeper."

And with this, he pulled himself out of the water. Ollie and Liberty simply stared at his side, mouths agape.

"What on earth's the matter with you two?" asked Specs.

The other two, not quite knowing how to inform Specs of the situation, could only manage to point limply at his side with their shaking little hands. As Specs looked down he almost stopped breathing. His whole arm had somehow disappeared.

"I told you it was dangerous!" Ollie finally exclaimed. "You wouldn't believe me."

Specs still couldn't quite believe what had happened. He simply stared in disbelief at his side, which was now quite definitely needing an arm back.

"I can't believe it" he said. "It felt so warm and nice in there, I could have stayed there all day."

"Well it's a good job you didn't" said Liberty crossly. "What if it had eaten you up completely?"

Ollie put his head in his hands and asked desperately, "How am I going to walk properly or skate or do anything now?"

For a while, Ollie and Specs in their different ways seemed heartbroken, and all Liberty could think to do was offer them one arm around each of their shoulders, while telling them not to worry and that they would think of something.

Chapter 4

In the days that followed both Ollie and Specs had to learn how to manage, one desperately wishing he had his foot back while the other couldn't help but reflect on how much easier life was with both his arms intact. Ollie limped around looking very sorry for himself for the first couple of days, but before long got back his zest for living and things felt reasonably normal again. Specs counted his blessings that he still had one good arm with which to hold Liberty, and as long as she was happy, so was he.

Each knew where the danger area was now and none of them dared to even get close again to the hole where Ollie's foot went through. Every day they nervously peered at it from a distance, fearful that somehow the stuff underneath the ice was going to come after them. In fact skating on the river at all was now completely banned in case anything like that were to happen again. It was a rule that none of them needed reminding about, however much it lessened their enjoyment. In fact their fear of the hole eventually created such a wide berth around it that their movement within the basin felt altogether tighter and more confined.

After several days of gradually getting used to this new life, Specs and Liberty were sitting together at the top of the basin under the shadow of the trees, a comfortable place from which to sit and observe their world, while Ollie was at the bottom of the bank making a whole batch of snowballs, ready for some enormous battle he was clearly planning for later that day. Ollie had made himself chief snowball maker, as Liberty wasn't a huge fan of snowball fights and found them all a bit unnecessary, and Specs found them awfully tricky to make without the assistance of his other arm, which he figured was still somewhere in the water, under the ice.

As the two sat on the higher ground, enjoying the spectacle of Ollie at work, an unusual sight caught Specs' eye on the leaf next to them. Their dear little caterpillar friend looked like he was trying to break out of his sleeping bag, the cocoon he had carefully woven around himself. Liberty's first urge was to try to help him, as he looked like he was finding it a little difficult, but Specs gently held her arm, sensing it was something he needed to do for himself.

As they continued to watch, something spellbinding began to take place. At first there was what seemed like a flash of colour. Then not just a flash of one colour, but a flash of many colours, vibrant and strong, as new organs and dimensions appeared to be slowly making their first movements, tentatively pushing the air and breaking their attachment to the old, now redundant, shell.

A few seconds later, and without any warning, a pair of beautiful tiny wings emerged majestically from behind his body, painted with what seemed like all the colours of the rainbow. Before Specs and Liberty had time to even look at each other to exchange expressions of awe and wonder, the once little green caterpillar had taken flight and now traversed the air, navigating through the gentle breeze, not like a beginner but like a creature immediately at one with the air, intimately knowing it as almost a part of itself.

For what seemed like an age, Specs and Liberty could say nothing, but followed it with their eyes until eventually it disappeared from their sight, into the beyond and away.

“Did you just see what I just saw?” asked Liberty.

“I thought perhaps I was dreaming” said Specs. “How on earth did it do that?”

Their enraptured faces were then startled by a sound from the sky above. As they looked up they saw a huge grey cloud loom over their basin, and suddenly, out of nowhere, little darts of something appeared to fill the air. Ollie immediately gave a terrified cry to them from below, chilling them to their very centre.

“It’s coming from the skies!”

From the top of the bank Specs anxiously shouted back to him, “What is?”

Ollie screamed again at the top of his voice, desperately trying to scramble up the bank to the safety and shelter of the trees.

"The stuff that took my foot and your arm! It's coming from the skies!"

As he said this, Liberty grabbed Specs and hauled him back under the branches.

"Quick!" screamed Liberty. "Hurry Ollie!"

Ollie began to run as fast as he could, dragging himself up the steep bank while each new dart of rain cut into his snowy body.

Then something very curious happened. As the rain continued to drive into his body, he gradually stopped trying to run and just stood in the rain. To Specs' and Liberty's amazement, a smile started to appear on his face as he looked up at the downpour pounding the white from his body. Baffled by what he could possibly be doing, his two friends screamed at him to join them under the safety of the trees, but Ollie remained in the rain with his arms outstretched, watching each drop go a little deeper into him each time. Over the merciless rain, Ollie shouted to his two friends: "You're right, Specs!"

"What?" Specs bellowed through the pouring rain, desperate to hear what his friend was trying to say.

"This stuff is strangely familiar" he added finally.

The rain was now beating and thrashing at their feet as they stood on the very edge of the tree's shelter, still frantically trying to reach Ollie with their pleas for him to find safety under the branches.

But Ollie wouldn't be moved. He simply stood there and allowed the rain little by little to lovingly transform the white of his body into a whole new form. Eventually, with the rain biting at their toes, poor Specs and Liberty were forced to retreat further back to where they could no longer even see their dear friend.

Chapter 5

When the rain had finally passed and they were sure they could no longer hear it, and as the familiar sounds of nature resumed, eventually they bravely surfaced from the trees and dared to look again toward where their dear friend had been. They took a deep breath and walked down the bank. Hand in hand they held each other tightly as they got closer, suddenly stopping with a gasp as they looked down. Ollie's scarf was now on the ground, but he was nowhere to be seen.

Liberty's voice quivered as she tried to speak.

"Where did he go? How could he just disappear like that?"

They kept Ollie's scarf by the trees, hoping that some day maybe he might come back and reclaim it. They figured that as they didn't actually know where he had gone, nor had they seen him disappear, maybe he might come back.

Barely a week had passed after the rain when, early one morning, as they were resting against their favourite tree, they were greeted by a sight on the skyline that they'd never seen before in their short lives: the brightest, most glorious golden sunrise imaginable.

"That is..." said Liberty, struggling for words. "That is..." But she couldn't finish her sentence.

"It's... beautiful. That's what you mean, isn't it?"

"It is that. It's very... that word" she said, still staring with awestruck wonder.

"Yes it is. Yes it is."

Both stood and watched it spellbound for what seemed like hours, as it rose higher and higher and began to beat down on them in the way sun does. Liberty soon found herself needing to loosen the scarf around her neck.

"It's making me feel strange" she said. "Like I want to take this thing off."

"Me too" said Specs quickly. "It's like nothing else I can think of."

The two friends on the bank basked in the glorious heat, lying down next to each other and looking up at the magnificent sun. They talked about what Ollie might have thought of this new thing they'd discovered. But before long the warmth of the sun's rays made them so drowsy that their conversation slowed to a stop, and soon they both dozed off.

Who knows how long they had been asleep, but finally Liberty shook Specs awake with alarm.

“Specs! Wake up!”

Specs jumped out of his skin and scrambled to his feet, ready to ask a reason for being woken so abruptly, but then looked around in disbelief, unable to believe what his eyes were telling him. During their sleep, parts of their dear basin, the only home they knew, had started to change colour. Instead of the usual snowy, white earth, patches all over the bank and bits at the bottom of it were starting to change to green. To poor Specs and Liberty, who had never yet met such a thing as grass, this was a frightening development. These unusual strands of green appeared suddenly to have taken up residence, like a surprise invasion, ousting the familiar white they’d grown used to with tremendous speed. They looked about them frantically to locate the remaining patches of still snowy ground, and found the nearest under the shade of the trees. In a great panic they got to their feet and rushed back into its shelter and protection. Liberty held tightly onto Specs as they hid as far into the shade as they could.

“Where’s the white gone?” asked poor Liberty, scared out of her wits. “Where’s it gone, Specs? It can’t just disappear... can it?”

"I don't know" said Specs anxiously. "But I'm more worried about that noise."

Liberty looked hardly able to even consider the prospect of anything more to worry about. Still, bravely they both took a deep breath and dared to look to where the noise was coming from. To their horror, at the bottom of the basin they saw water gushing into the river from all directions.

“It’s that stuff... from the sky... from under the ice. Look at it all, it’s everywhere” gasped Liberty, trembling terribly.

As the sun continued to beat down, they were deafened by the unrelenting noise of their surroundings melting and meeting the river.

“What’s happening to us, Specs?” asked Liberty with a sorrowful little sniffle. “This place is nothing like it used to be.”

“It’ll be okay, I’m sure it will” Specs assured her, as confidently as he could.

“We’re getting smaller, you know, or our noses are getting bigger.”

“Yes, I know” said Specs, as though confessing something that he’d been secretly aware of for a while.

“I don’t think I’m very pretty anymore” said Liberty with a sob. “Not half as nice as when I first met you.”

“You’re even more lovely now” Specs quickly reassured her.

“But today some of my hair fell out” she added.

“Who needs hair?” said Specs.

Specs and Liberty didn’t move from the shelter and shade of the trees for the rest of the morning and even into the afternoon. In fact, it was hard enough even to dare to look out, as every time they did, a little more of their dear home, the basin, had disappeared, taken over by new armies of the strange green stuff. The islands of white were becoming smaller and smaller, and the golden sun that had seemed so beautiful earlier, now seemed harsh and unrelenting. They didn’t know how, but they knew that it had somehow joined forces and was working on the side of the thing they feared most, the water.

Under the tree they huddled together against the thick trunk and watched throughout the day, as the circle of shade around them shifted its shape with the movement of the sun, at first seeming to offer them ample protection, but then slowly, as the afternoon wore on, contracting, and pushing them tighter and tighter against the tree. At one point, without even realising it, Liberty found her little foot poking out from the boundary of the shade into the full glare of the sun. She then realised something even more terrifying. She froze and nudged Specs.

“Look” she whispered.

Specs, looking down at her exposed little foot, saw that a small pool of water had gathered right against it. He couldn't help but look aghast, but then quickly composed himself and tried not to show this to poor Liberty. In the calmest manner he could manage, he whispered to her:
"Don't make any sudden movements. Just very slowly move your foot in."

Liberty did so, leaving the little pool of water beyond the shade, seeming to stare at them menacingly.

"Where did it come from?" she asked. "I didn't even see it creep up on us."

Something in Liberty's last words seemed to send Specs deep into thought. He paused, as though suddenly wrestling with an extraordinary idea.

"Maybe it didn't" he said finally.

"What do you mean?" she asked.

"Come around here" he said, with unusual authority.

Specs moved to the other side of the tree, away from the water and where the boundary of the shade was now closest to them. Liberty, although apprehensive and not entirely happy with this plan, faithfully agreed, initially at least, and went with him.

“When I say so, we’re both going to put one foot outside the shade into the brightness” Specs said resolutely.

“I don’t think that’s a terribly good idea” Liberty said, in her most polite but firm voice.

Specs looked at her with a pitiful little expression, imploring her to trust him. Finally, her devotion to him won and she couldn’t help herself.

“Okay.”

Holding hands, they each slowly poked one of their little feet out into the glare of the sun. For a moment there was nothing; a moment longer, still nothing. But then, as they continued to watch and as the sun worked its magic, they began to notice the white of their feet seeming to sweat. To their amazement and wonder, small beads of water started to gather on the surface of each foot,

like little pearls that had always been hidden deep within the shells of their snowy bodies.

Neither could think what to say, and both remained speechless as the pearls started to trickle down their feet onto the green of the earth outside the shade. To begin with the drops seemed to disappear into the earth without a trace; but before long, once the earth had been sufficiently quenched, a little circle of water began to appear next to each foot, just like the one before. Liberty was mesmerised by the sight of her own little pool.

“That’s me” she said, like a little child recognising itself for the first time in a mirror.

“Yes” said Specs, smiling. “And here I am” he continued, pointing at the circle next to his own foot.

With their hands still tightly clenched, they watched as each pool gradually swelled and pushed its boundary toward the other, until there came a moment that neither Specs nor Liberty had anticipated. The two pools, on a seemingly unstoppable course toward each other, first kissed, and then merged seamlessly into each other.

For a few seconds neither could think of anything that needed to be said. Everything was becoming clear and beautiful, and the fear that had gripped them for so long, that was almost a part of them, started to release its grip. To them both, the world now seemed full of possibilities.

“We’re... the same stuff... exactly the same” Liberty finally articulated.

“Yes” said Specs, hardly able to speak.

“How do we know where I end and you begin?” said Liberty, looking at the single pool of water before them.

“We don’t” said Specs, as if seeing something for the first time. “That’s the beauty of it.”

Liberty turned to Specs as his voice began to crack, and saw more of the same pearls start to gather in the whites of his eyes, behind his spectacles, before trickling down his face, forging everlasting furrows down his pale cheeks.

“It was inside us all the time” said Liberty.

Specs nodded, smiling. Then she too began to feel a swelling in the sockets of her own little acorn eyes. And soon they could no longer hold their cargo of tears, which finally ran down her soft white face. Liberty looked out again at their dear basin.

“The sun seems beautiful again” she said, almost to herself and with a note of surprise.

“Yes it does. Yes it does” agreed Specs.

Chapter 6

Several months had passed since the sun first visited the basin. Back in the little town that lived beyond the hill from the circle of trees, little Alice remembered their creations and tried to convince her brothers to come with her back to the basin. In her young heart, she still hoped that by some miracle the figures would still be there.

Although her older brothers loved their little sister to bits, they couldn't help teasing her innocent, magical heart a little, telling her it would be a wasted journey. Undaunted, little Alice set off on her own, over the hill to the circle of trees in the distance. The sun accompanied her for the whole journey, warming her gently as she walked.

Gradually the trees, which had seemed so far away to start with, no bigger than her thumb when she held it up, slowly got larger and larger, until finally her destination was upon her. Excitedly, she quickly ascended to the top of the steep bank and stared down into the basin beneath, beaming with hopeful expectation.

Slowly but surely, the innocent smile began to fade from her face, as beneath her all that her little eyes could see was the green, green grass and the flow of the river beyond it.

With a heavy heart, she slowly descended into the basin and sat by the river's edge. As a tear rolled down her cheek, she was forced to agree that her brothers were right, that she was a silly little girl with too big an imagination. Their beautiful creations were never going to be still there. Hardly able to consider the long journey back with such an empty heart, she got up and began to walk slowly back up the steep bank.

Then, somewhere between the water's edge and the trees at the top, she suddenly noticed on the ground her mother's best silk scarf, bought from the Liberty boutique in London, and right next to it an old pair of her grandad's spectacles. The corner of her mouth turned up into a little half smile, as through the sadness, a memory full of love came flooding back.

Putting the treasures carefully into her pocket, she continued to the top of the bank, where to her surprise she found her brother Oliver's scarf next to one of the trees. She wondered how on earth it had got so far from her mother's scarf and the spectacles. Then her eyes were drawn, as if magically, to the heart that Ollie had inscribed at the base of the tree with the flint – a heart encasing their names, Specs, Liberty and Ollie, that marked their beloved basin as home.

With a rush of excitement she could hardly contain, Alice grappled in her pocket for her mother's scarf and searched for the label. On seeing LIBERTY embossed on it in gold letters her heart began to jump for joy. She quickly delved into her pocket for her grandad's spectacles and looked at them again, with fresh eyes, her mind now starting to make the connections as her lips silently mouthed the word 'Specs', with a smile so bright it dashed all her sorrow away.

As she looked back at the inscribed heart surrounding their names, she knew they had been friends, and that they had lived, and somewhere still lived. Her journey back had all the energy and excitement of the first day of winter.

As Specs and Liberty had found their wings and together with Ollie had joined the river, so the river had joined the ocean, and as the ocean evaporated, as an ocean does, and was taken up into the clouds, finally it returned over the basin and rained back down onto its branches the ounce of spirit that had only ever been borrowed for the play. Specs, Liberty and Ollie had finally returned from whence they came. And the trees smiled.

Soon winter would be here again and there would be more snow and more adventures.

The End